I0021854

Factors Affecting in Information Behavior of Managers in the Nepalese Civil Service

An Empirical Study of Civil Servants in Nepal

Binaya Hari Maskey

ELIVA PRESS

Binaya Hari Maskey

The importance of context in information seeking is a growing concerned in the emerging literature. The objective of this study is to understand the impact of personal and professional factors on information behavior of Nepalese Civil Services (NCS) Officers/Managers.

Regarding methodology, the study was followed quantitative research and data were collected through the distribution of structured survey questionnaire in the non-contrived settings. Time horizon of this study is a cross-sectional. The unit of analysis is in-service employees of NCS. Accordingly, data were captured using a structured questionnaire sent to a total 155 NSC Officers, out of which 84 questionnaires were collected, which is above 54% achievement obtained in the response rate. Data Analysis were conducted using MS Excel and statistical analysis package (SPSS 21vr.). Descriptive and inferential statistical analysis like frequencies, percentage, ANOVA, MANOVA; and multiple comparisons with the Scheffe test were also conducted to examine the proposed hypotheses.

The finding of the study showed that the demographic personal factors like age and the organisational/professional factors like job experience and information system use are only the contextual variables, which make a difference in the all three elements of information dimensions (or IB). This means, therefore, both null hypothesis (H0) and alternative hypothesis (H1) have been only partially supported. Hence, it can be concluded from the study findings that Nepalese Civil Service Officers/Managers' personal and professional factors do create differences in their IB. However, the low sample size is one of the major limitations of this study.

Published by Eliva Press SRL
Address: MD-2060, bd.Cuza-Voda, 1/4, of. 21 Chişinău, Republica
Moldova
Email: info@elivapress.com
Website: www.elivapress.com

ISBN: 978-1-63648-123-4

Factors Affecting in Information Behavior of Managers in the Nepalese Civil Service (An Empirical Study of Civil Servants in Nepal)

Binaya Hari Maskey

Nepal Administrative Staff College (NASC), Jawalakhel, Nepal

E-mail:- **bhmaskey@gmail.com**

Abstract

The importance of context in information seeking is a growing concerned in the emerging literature. The objective of this study is to understand the impact of personal and professional factors on information behavior of Nepalese Civil Services (NCS) Officers/Managers.

Regarding methodology, the study was followed quantitative research and data were collected through the distribution of structured survey questionnaire in the non-contrived settings. Time horizon of this study is a cross-sectional. The unit of analysis is in-service employees of NCS. Accordingly, data were captured using a structured questionnaire sent to a total 155 NSC Officers, out of which 84 questionnaire were collected, which is above 54% achievement obtained in the response rate. Data Analysis were conducted using MS Excel and statistical analysis package (SPSS 21vr.). Descriptive and inferential statistical analysis like frequencies, percentage, ANOVA, MANOVA; and multiple comparisons with the Scheffe test were also conducted to examine the proposed hypotheses.

The finding of the study showed that the demographic personal factors like age and the organisational/ professional factors like job experience and information system use are only the contextual variables, which make a difference in the all three elements of information dimensions (or IB). This means, therefore, both null hypothesis (H0) and alternative hypothesis (H1) have been only partially supported. Hence, it can be concluded from the study findings that Nepalese Civil Service Officers/Managers' personal and professional factors do create differences in their IB. However, the low sample size is one of the major limitations of this study.

Key Words: Information Behaviour, Information Seeking, Nepalese Civil Service, information contexts, Demographic Personal Factors, Demographic Professional Factors, Information Characteristics, Information Sources, Information Types.

Table of Contents

Contents

1. Introduction

Background

Information Behavior (IB) came from concept of importance of information (i.e. dealing with information needs and usage). IB describes how a manager need, seeks, manage & exchange information in different situation according to their context of requirements, either that are intentional information seeking or unintentional information encounters (Case, Information behavior, 2006, p. 294). It is also known as (a.k.a.) information-seeking behavior or human information behavior. IB was coined in the late 1990s, however began in the 1960s. Now a days, the importance of context in information seeking is a growing concerned in the emerging literature.

The importance of context in information seeking[1] is a growing concerned in the emerging literature. Case (2007, p. 13) has defined context in information behavior as "the particular combination of person and situation that serve[s] to frame an investigation" of information behavior. According to him (Case, 2007), there are three types of contexts that are commonly studied in information behavior. They are known as occupation, social role, and demographic groupings.

Scholars of information behavior acknowledge that there is no single theory of information seeking as such (Case, 2007, p. 148). Information behavior approaches are typically regarded as models because they focus on specific problems (Case, 2007, p. 120).

Any organizations operating in open social systems, whether that are within organizational level or managerial level, in the both conditions the importance of information emerges from the necessity of dealing with *uncertainty*. According to Thompson, uncertainty is the "*fundamental problem of complex organization and coping with uncertainty is the essence of administrative* process" (Thompson, 1967, p.

---

[1] Information Seeking is "a conscious effort to acquire information in response to a need or gap" in your knowledge (https://liswiki.org/wiki/Information_behavior_theories).

159). According to him, there are two major sources of uncertainty. They are technology and environment.

Now days, these two sources of uncertainty (i.e. technology and environment) are becoming more complex and dynamic in nature and thus has been changing constantly. It indicates the propensity of the degree of uncertainty is growing rapidly. In other to survive and to grow in such a situation of uncertainly, every organizations need to increase their information-processing capacity. Most of the researchers have argued that the organization has limited information-processing capacity [(Simon, 1960); (Swanson, 2003)].

To increase this capacity, organizations need to increase managers' information management skills (collecting, analyzing, and transmitting), which obviously means to enhance managers' information behavior (Almutairi, 2011).

Besides this, it is indispensable to know what contextual factors influence on managerial information behavior. That is because, these may obstruct or construct this type of behavior. Lack of the understanding of these factors may kept managers in the black box and they could not understand how to control their information behavior, which is indispensable in todays' emerging uncertainty and competitive and dynamic business environment that is built around information (Almutairi, 2011). It is equally applicable in profit and non-profit or service motive organisations.

Several research studies [(Paisley, 1968); (Auster & Choo, 1993); Losch and Lambert, 2007, as cited in (Almutairi, 2011)] relating to the contextual factors affecting the information behavior shown that the studied groups either have not fast enough to keep up with the speed of information technologies and information society changes or there is a paucity of knowledge on how managers acquire and use information in their work and more surprisingly found that the conceptualization and nature of information behavior are still not clear.

In addition, during the last three decades, literature showed that several empirical investigations [(Auster & Choo, 1993); (Palsdottir, 2003); (Hupfer & Detlor, 2006);

(Lorence & Park, 2007); (Williams & Coles, 2007); (Urquhart & Yeoman, 2009); (Robinson, 2010)] have been conducted to understand the impact of contextual factors in terms of personal and professional variables in the various information behaviour dimensions and found that personal and professional characteristics do make a difference in information behaviour. However, looking at these empirical studies, it is also noticed that most of these studies focused on only parts of the information behavior.

As a result, information behavior is a concept that researchers, academicians, HR managers, policy makers, decision makers and concerned professional & practitioners still need to focus on. That is because, this is one of the core factor that distinguishes between success and failure in the newly emerging competitive business environment.

In addition, there is no research on this topic in Nepalese context using the related affecting variables (such as demographic factor or personal variables; and organizational factor like professional variables). Thus, the research aims at filling the knowledge gap on this area in our country's context and to motivate other Nepalese scholars to include and expand other affecting variables which leads to enhance future research work in the field.

This research finding will help to increase the knowledge on how Nepalese managers acquire and use information in their work; and also helps to improve and increase the Nepalese Managers' information-processing capacity; so that they will be fast enough to keep up with the speed of IT and information society changes. This means, the organisation will be able to survive and growth in the degree of uncertainly. In addition, this study might help to formulate or refine existing strategies.

Statement of the Problem

Importance of information emerges from the necessity of dealing with uncertainty. Uncertainty is the fundamental problem of complex organization and coping with it is the essence of administrative process. Major sources of uncertainty are Technology and Environment (Thompson, 1967, p. 159). These are becoming more complex, dynamic & changing constantly. Thus, the degree of uncertainty is becoming very high.

To be able to survive and growth in such degree of uncertainly, organizations need to increase their information-processing capacity. However, several researchers have argued that the organization has limited information-processing capacity [(Simon, 1960); (Swanson, 2003)]. It is also not an exception in the context of government organizations including other Nepalese organisations in Nepal as well. Thus, to increase this capacity, organizations need to increase managers' information management skills (i.e. collecting, analyzing, and transmitting). This means, they need to enhance managers' IB (Almutairi, 2011), which is equally applicable in profit and non-profit or service motive organisations as well as in the Nepalese context, too.

In addition, it is indispensable to know what contextual factors effect on managerial information behavior because these may obstruct or enhance this type of behavior. Lack of the understanding of these contextual factors keeps managers in the dark area concerning to how to control their information behavior, which is essential in todays' emerging uncertainty, competitive and dynamic business environment which is built around information (Almutairi, 2011).

Previous Researches and findings also highlight these facts. In 1968, Paisley's; In 1993, Auster and Choo; and more recently, in 2007, Losch and Lambert researches [(Paisley, 1968); (Auster & Choo, 1993); Losch and Lambert, 2007, as cited in (Almutairi, 2011)] showed that the studied groups either have not fast enough to keep up with the speed of information technologies and information society changes or there is a paucity of knowledge on how managers acquire and use information in their work. They also argued that the conceptualization and nature of information behavior are still not clear.

Research Question

Therefore, based on the study background, problem statement, and in other to enhance knowledge regarding the significance of this area in the Nepalese Civil Service

Officers/managers and Nepalese management, the present study will mainly attempt to answer the following general question:

Do Nepalese Civil Service Officers/ Managers' Demographic Personal and Professional Factors Create Differences in Their Information Behaviour?

2. Literature Review

Theoretical Framework

From the relevant and currently available literature review on "information behavior" has revealed that there has been gradual shift of research interest in the information behavior research since 1970s. From the year, study began to shift from a system orientation to a user orientation (Case, 2007). In other word, its contemporary research and scholars have stressed their potential on the individual as information seeker and user.

The importance of context in information seeking[2] is a growing concerned in the emerging literature. Case (2007, p. 13) has defined context in information behavior as "the particular combination of person and situation that serve(s) to frame an investigation" of information behavior. According to him (Case, 2007), there are three types of contexts that are commonly studied in information behavior. They are known as occupation, social role, and demographic groupings.

Case (2007) argued in his review of information behaviour research, that human information behaviour is more complex and interpersonal than it was assumed before. He stressed that context is the most significant themes among others in current information behaviour research and that can be examined and tested by adding demographic and organisatioal factors. The chaotic nature of information behaviour is a tip off the complexity of the environment and that urged to include more variables in

---

[2] Information Seeking is "a conscious effort to acquire information in response to a need or gap" in your knowledge (https://liswiki.org/wiki/Information_behavior_theories).

our study to explain this behaviour. These could be personal variables, such as age, sex, and education, and work-related variables, such as experience, task, and structure can play a vital role in shaping behaviour.

Wilson [(1981); and (1999)] has provided a series of models of information seeking and information behaviour and presented a generic conceptual framework of information behaviour. According to Wilson, need for information triggers information behavior, which subsequently related to three main sequential process known as seeking information, exchanging information, and using information. These process of activities are repeated till the information need of a person is satisfied. He argued that information needs can be original and or secondary ones, which is rooted from basic needs. These are related to Maslow's Hierarchy of Needs as physiological, safety, social, esteem, self-actualization, which are mainly related to cognitive, or affecting.

These basic needs could influence_by several other contextual factors such as profession, occupation (or task within which the work and life take place), social and environmental (political, economic, technological, etc.) role, and personal variables (i.e. age, gender, education), and so on. Likewise, situation-specific need, frequency (recurring or new need), predictability (anticipated or unexpected need), importance (degrees of urgency), and complexity (easily resolved or difficult), etc., characteristics also determine the information needs of a person(s) (Leckie, Pettigrew, & Sylvain, 1996). According to Leckie and his colleagues, information needs create from the situations pertaining to a specific task that is associated with one or more of the work roles played by the professional. They also found that other factors like individual demographics and organisatioal attributes and circumstances, such as age, profession, specialisation, career stage, and geographic location has also influenced professionals' information needs. Beside these, Wilson (1999), cautioned that, barriers to information search will emerge from the same set of contexts or the situations pertaining to a specific task and characteristics.

Review of the literature of several scholars of different periods related to information behavior have shown that information seeking and use depends on various factors such as subject faculties, profession, activities, situation, and context [(Wilson T. , 1981); (Wilson T. , 1999); (Wilson T. D., 2000); (Case, 2006); (Case, 2007); (Bates, 2010); (Savolainen, 2007)], and [also see in (Rice & Tarin, 1993); (Solomon, 1997); (Dervin, 1997); (Borgman, 2006); (Kling & McKim, 2000); (Cool, 2001); (Hansen & Järvelin, 2005); (Vakkari, 2006), as cited in Wikipedia].

Scholars developed several principles and proposed at both in depth and breadth levels of detail studies [eg. Zipf's principle of least effort; Brenda Dervin's sense making, 2005; Stuart Card, Ed H. Chi and Peter Pirolli's Information foraging; Elfreda Chatman's life in the round; Wilson's model of information behavior, 1981, 1999; Nicholas J. Belkin's episodic model and Anomalous state of knowledge (ASK), 1980; David Ellis's six and eight key activities that identified in the information seeking process; Carol Kuhlthau's Information search process (ISP), 1993; as cited in Wikipedia[3]], while exploring to understand the processes in the domain of information seeking and/or information behavior.

In the same way, additional theories and models of information behaviour have also drawn attention to the impact of specific contextual variables. As for example, Bystrom's (2006) theory of information activities in work tasks, Taylor's (1991, as cited in (Almutairi, 2011) theory of information use environments, and theory of work task information-seeking and retrieval processes developed by Hansen [(2006), as cited in (Almutairi, 2011)] also confirmed to the theory of information behaviour.

Finally, information behaviour theories has raised the issue of the importance of context in forming information behavior as it raised in human behaviour theories. Supporting on this issue, Mick *et al.* (1980, as cited in (Almutairi, 2011) stressed that information travels through complex paths and information behaviour is the product of a complex interaction of several factors such as personal factors, environment, and task. In addition, he argued that there is a rare case that the same information behaviour is expressed by two individuals; thus, he again stated that information_behaviour

---

[3] https://en.wikipedia.org/w/index.php?title=Information_seeking_behavior&action=edit

improvement intervention should focus on specific situations and factors that can be controlled, such as variables within organizational boundaries.

Thus, in conclusion, scholars of information behavior acknowledge that there is no single theory of information seeking as such (Case, 2007, p. 148). Information behavior approaches are typically regarded as models because they focus on specific problems (Case, 2007, p. 120).

Study done in Personal and Professional factors

Literature shows that, several empirical investigations have been conducted during the last three decades to understand the impact of personal and professional variables in the various information behaviour dimensions. Scholar Palsdottir and other scholars argued that the sex of the respondent makes a difference in information behavior [(Palsdottir, 2003); (Urquhart & Yeoman, 2009)]. Kenkel and his contemporary scholars' studies have found that women are more active with health information than men [Kenkel, 1990; Rutten, L. J., Squiers, L., & Hesse, B. 2006, as cited in (Almutairi, 2011); (Lorence & Park, 2007)]. The research results of the Hupfer and Detlor (2006) shown that compare to the men, women are greater information seekers.

While examining demographic and organisational variables (i.e. experiences in current organization, age, and sex) influence on the choice of media selection by new managers, who handle HR problems, Barnard [(1991), as cited in (Almutairi, 2011), found from his research study that new managers in the service sector use business_mail more frequently than their counterparts in other sectors of organizations. Besides that, for obtaining information, younger managers (< 40 ages) were found participated more often in social activities as information sources and they found subordinates and peers more useful more often than older and senior managers did. Similarly, male managers also use subordinates as information sources compare to the female managers did. The reasons of these outcomes, according to the researcher Barnard might be the cause of experience they had in dealing with them and hence feel comfortable in using them as information sources. The researcher argued that young managers' use of subordinates as information sources might be a reflection of a trend towards an open management style.

Above empirical evidence aptly shows that personal and professional characteristics do make a difference in information behaviour. However, looking at these empirical studies we notice that most of these studies focused on only parts of the information behaviour, which included information sources [Barnard 1991; as cited in (Almutairi, 2011); (Robinson, 2010)], impact of gender of respondent in information behavior [Kenkel 1990; Rutten et al. 2006, as cited in (Almutairi, 2011), (Palsdottir, 2003); (Hupfer & Detlor, 2006); (Lorence & Park, 2007); (Urquhart & Yeoman, 2009)], in frequency of use [Larner 2006; Pors 2008, as cited in (Almutairi, 2011)], and information usage and choice of information source [(Auster & Choo, 1993); (Williams & Coles, 2007); (Robinson, 2010)].

Conceptual framework

For our study to view information behaviour and factors impacting upon it as a complex phenomenon that involves several types of factors and relationships in the context of current Nepalese Civil Service Officers/Managers in Government of Nepal (GoN), following diagram has attempted to summarize the conceptual model. (see in *Figure 1: The Study Model*) (Almutairi, 2011).

Such a conceptual model would lead to knowing which relationship, or part thereof, could enhance or obstruct informational activities. This is one of this model's purposes. Second, this study attempts to help in doing validation of the previous propositions and empirical findings by investigating information behaviour of non-Western managers and, more specifically, Civil Service Officers/Managers in GoN, thereby enhancing the generalization of those findings.

The Study model

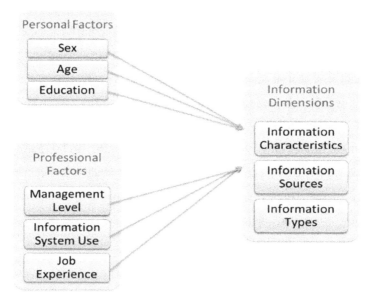

Figure 1: The Study Model

3. Research Objectives

Primary Objective

The main objective of the study is to understand the impact of personal and professional factors on information behavior of Nepalese Civil Services Officers/Managers. In other words, this study will enhance managers' information behavior through advancing our knowledge of the factors affecting their behaviors. More precisely, this study investigates these factors in the context of Nepalese Civil Services Officers.

Secondary Objectives

Second, this study attempts to help in doing validation of the previous model (Almutairi, 2011) and propositions by undertaking empirical research investigation, that is through finding information behaviour of non-Western managers and, more specifically, Civil Service Officers/Managers in GoN, thereby enhancing the generalization of those findings.

14

4. Research Hypothesis

Based on the above review following hypotheses were developed:

H_0: The personal and professional background factors of the NCS Officers/Managers do not create difference or impact in their Information Behaviour (i.e. Information Dimensions);

H_1: The factors of personal background (i.e. gender, age, education) of NCS Officers/Managers and/or their factors of professional background (i.e. management class/level, job experience, information system use at work) do create difference or impact in their Information Behaviour (i.e. Information Dimensions, particularly in information characters, information sources and information systems use).

5. Methodology

Research Design

For this research study, researcher has used a relational model developed by (Almutaiii, 2011). The main purpose & usage of the study model is to examine the relationships between the managers' demographic and organisational (i.e. personal and professional) factors and their information behaviour. This familiarize with, which relationship, or part thereof, could enhance or obstruct in their informational activities/behaviour. This is a quantitative research; therefore, survey questionnaire method has been used to collect the required information in the non-contrived settings. Time horizon of this study is a cross-sectional. The unit of analysis is in-service employees of NCS.

The model is empirically tested with 155 NSC managers/officers using the customized structured survey questionnaire of Almutaire (2011) techniques, out of which total 84 questionnaire were collected, which is above 54% achievement obtained in the response rate. The questionnaire has been divided into four sections. Section A were designed to collect information characteristics dimension; Section B were incorporated information types dimensions; Section C were included information source dimensions and Section D were covered demographical and organisational information (i.e. relating to personal and professional information).

Population & Sampling, Data Collection Method

Data have been collected using a questionnaire sent to a total sample size of 155 Managers/Officers, who are currently working and/or available within the Kathmandu Valley. In total 84 questionnaire were collected out of 155 questionnaire distributed, which is above 54% achievement obtained in the response rate. From the collected questionnaire, 5 has been eliminated because the participants either provided two answers for the same question or left most of the questions unanswered, leaving only 79 were found usable questionnaire (50% of the total distributed questionnaire) for data analysis. In the distribution of the questionnaire, researcher has attempted to include both male and female of different age groups from different work nature and different backgrounds while obtaining samples, so that a variety of data can be collected. A convenient sampling technique has been used for data collection.

The detail characteristics of the sample were mentioned in the Table-1, as shown in following page. The table shown that 15% (i.e. 12) of the respondents found female while 85% (i.e. 67) found male. More than 50% (i.e. 40) were 41 years or older, while only 5% (i.e. 4) found below 30 years old. In addition, nearly 70% (i.e. 55) had Master degree and one respondent hold a PhD degree, which reported that most officers hold higher than the minimum required (i.e. graduate) degrees. In other words, this had also indicated that educational aspect of majority of the officers in NCS sector might have a good level of qualification. Likewise, more than 60% (i.e. 48) of the respondents had already served in the NCS sector for more than 15 years, but only 15% (i.e. 12) had served between 6 to 10 years in NCS. As against this, only 2 out of 79 respondents had served in the NCS sector for just below 5 years only. It seems there may be significantly low proportionate of new comer officers in NCS. Concerning the respondents' managerial level/class, 73% (i.e. 58) were junior level (i.e. class III) managers, whereas only 26% (i.e. 21) were middle Class Officer. Similarly, about 50% (i.e. 39) of the respondents highlighted that their usage of information system in their official tasks related work were used at moderate level, in the same context, it shown here that more than 31% (i.e. 25) had used at good level. These figure shown that IS use at work is at satisfactory level. Another point to be noted here is that although there were very low percent or few respondents shown in weak and excellent level of IS used at work (i.e. 5 and 10 respondents), comparing between these two weak levels, excellent level of IS used at work has poorest condition (i.e. 6.3% only), which indicated that we need to do further improvement in IS use at work at earliest possible, so that percentage of excellent level in this factor (i.e. IS use) can be increased. This will only be possible when, offices run new advance and/or upgraded ICT based IS in its offices and simultaneously provide ICT skill based trainings to its employees in regular basis.

Table-1: Descriptive Properties of Demographic elements

Characteristics		Frequency	Percent	Cumulative Percent
Gender				
	Male	67	84.8	84.8
	Female	12	15.2	100
	Total	79	100	
Age				
	Under 30	4	5.1	5.1
	30 to 40	35	44.3	49.4
	41 or older	40	50.6	100
	Total	79	100	
Class				
	II	21	26.6	26.6
	III	58	73.4	100
	Total	79	100	
Education				
	PhD	1	1.3	1.3
	Master	55	69.6	69.6
	Graduate	22	27.8	100
	Total	79	100	
Total Service Year				
	5 years or less	2	2.5	2.5
	6 to 10 years	12	15.2	17.7
	11 to 15 years	17	21.5	39.2
	16 to 20 years	31	39.2	78.5
	21 years or more	17	21.5	100
	Total	79	100	
Level of IS Used at Work				
	Excellent	5	6.3	6.3

	Good	25	31.6	38
	Moderate	39	49.4	87.3
	Weak	10	12.7	100
	Total	79	100	

Note:- The table format of the SPSS OUTPUT has been slightly modified for the readability & simplicity;

Surveyed questionnaire has been divided into four sections i.e. section A, B, C & D. In the Section **A** included Information Characteristics Dimension, which measures using ten information characteristics. In the Section **B** of the questionnaire, there has been designed to collect information types dimension, which was measured using four general information types i.e. general information about the organization, information about the employees, information about the customers/cliental, and information about organizational plans and procedures all together in 15 statements. In the Section **C** of the questionnaire, the information source dimension related information was attempted to collect, which was measured using twenty-eight information sources within three categories (i.e. traditional source, electronic source, personal source). Finally, in the Section **D** of the questionnaire has been designed to collect demographical information (i.e. personal and professional information) that includes six person-related variables: age, sex, education, management level, job experience and information system use.

Variables and Measures

The information characteristics and information types dimension were measured using a five-point Likert-type scale responses ranged from 1 (no importance/ very high disagreement) to 5 (very high importance/ very high agreement). The information sources dimension were measured using Yes/No responses to indicate the usage of the information sources. A convenient sampling technique has been used for data collection. Above mentioned all information dimension variable types, which were used in the present study have already been tested by other researchers, too [e.g., (Ashill & Jobber, 2001); (O'Reilly, 1982); (Breen, 2005); (Koksal, 2008)], thus, assumed that the reliability and validity measurement of those variables are satisfactory.

In all cases, alpha (significance value) is set at 0.05, to test at the 5% significance level. In other to assess the reliability of each scaled measure, Cronbach's alpha was used for the three information behaviour dimensions. The calculated Cronbach's alpha coefficients values for information characteristics, information types and information sources were 0.827, 0.916 and 0.874, respectively (see in Table-2 in the following page). A normative standard value of Cronbach's alpha for the acceptable level of reliability is fixed at 0.70 Hair et al. (2009, as cited in (Sudin, 2011)) and (Nunnally, 1967, as cited in (Almutairi, 2011)] and was adopted in this study.

Table-2: Reliability Statistics

Variables	Cronbach's Alpha	No. of Items
Information Characteristic	0.827	10
Information Type	0.916	15
Information Source	0.874	25

Data Analysis

Data analysis was done using the MS Excel and statistical analysis package known as SPSS 21vr., to carry out data entries, various analysis and test like frequency distribution, cross tabulations, multivariate analysis of variance (MANOVA), analysis of variance (ANOVA), and multiple comparisons with the Scheffe test and so on. These statistical methods were used in this study, mainly because, these were useful to obtain different types of outputs from each statistical methods in terms of wideness and/or scope of the output.

6. Results and Interpretation of the Results

Presentation and Descriptive Analysis of Data

The primary objective of the study is to advancing our knowledge of personal and professional factors affecting on information behavior of Nepalese Civil Services Officers/Managers. To properly address this objective, the study examined to find out that information behavior (i.e. need, seek, exchange and use of information dimensions such as characteristics, types and sources of information) of Nepalese Civil Services

Officers in different work roles that whether their personal and professional traits may obstruct or support information seeking.

Factors Affecting in Information Characteristics

After close study of the Chart-1 of Table-6b as shown in the following pages, we can draw result that among the ten information characteristics, timeliness, specificity, clarity, trustworthiness, unbiased, Usefulness and truthfulness have shown that more than 70% of its' respondents measured these information characteristics on high importance and very high importance ratings. Thus, it can be concluded that, these information characteristics could have significant impact on information behaviour of NCS Officers/Managers. As against these compare to above characteristics, subjectivity and flexibility have found given comparatively lowest priority by assigning least ratings by the respondents on high importance and very high importance ratings (i.e. by assigning ratings mainly on important ratings only). However, if we include importance rating too, the result have also shown that respondents measured all ten information characteristics at more than 75%. This indicated that all ten information characteristics could have significant impact on information behaviour of NCS Officers/Managers, too. Furthermore, three information characteristics namely trustworthiness, unbiased and flexibility were found 2.5, 5.1 and 2.5 percentage of non-respondent, which were not significantly influence in the study.

Factors Affecting in Information Types

From the detail examination of the Chart-2 of Table-7b as shown in the following pages (which were drawn from Table-7b), we can draw result that the information types indicated by the respondents were quite moderate. It is because, in among the fifteen statements related to four types of information (i.e. employee, Org. plans & procedure, client and general org. information), the trend of rating selection in the chart have shown that in an average more than 73% of the respondents selected their ratings mainly on agreement and high agreement applicable for all four types of information and/or in their related statements. It has also shown that none of the respondents mentioned their ratings on very high disagreement level. Regarding the nonrespondents, in an average only 3% were found (see in Chart-3 & 4 of Table-8b as shown in the following pages, too) and its major portion lies in information related to the Client type information/statements only (i.e. between 6% to 8% for this particular information type). Again, Chart-3 and Chart-4 of Table-8b as shown in the following

Chart-1 of Table-6b: Respondents' Ratings on Information Characteristics

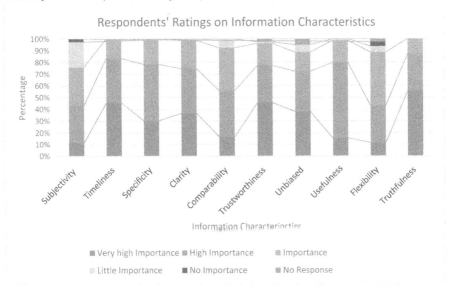

Table-6b: Percentage of Information Characteristics

Percentage of Information Characteristics :

Information Characteristics	Very high Importance	High Importance	Importance	Little Importance	No Importance	No Response	Very High and High Importance	Very High and High and Importance
Subjectivity	11.4	31.6	32.9	21.5	2.5		43.0	75.9
Timeliness	45.6	38.0	16.5				83.5	100.0
Specificity	30.4	48.1	21.5				78.5	100.0
Clarity	36.7	38.0	24.1	1.3			74.7	98.7
Comparability	16.5	39.2	36.7	7.6			55.7	92.4
Trustworthiness	45.6	31.6	19.0	1.3		2.5	77.2	96.2
Unbiased	38.0	34.2	16.5	6.3		5.1	72.2	88.6
Usefulness	15.2	64.6	19.0	1.3			79.7	98.7
Flexibility	11.4	31.6	45.6	5.1	3.8	2.5	43.0	88.6
Truthfulness	55.7	31.6	12.7				87.3	100.0

21

pages, also conformed the above finding and thus shown that in an average 73% of its respondents selected their ratings in moderate range (i.e. agreement and high agreement). Thus, it can be concluded that, all four type of information might have significant impact on information behaviour of Nepalese Civil Services Officers/Managers.

Chart-2 of Table-7b: Respondents' Ratings on Information Types & Related Statements

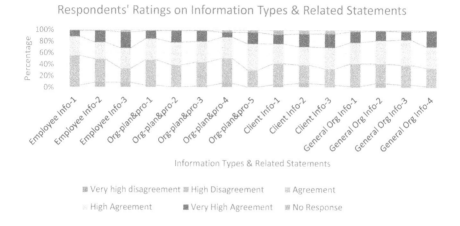

Table-7b: Percentage of Types of Information
(Respondents' Ratings on Information Types & Related Statements)

Inform ation Types	Very high disagreement	High Disagreem ent	Agree ment	High Agreeme nt	Very High Agreement	No Resp onse	Agree ment & High Agree ment
Emplo yee Info-1		3.8	51.9	32.9	10.1	1.3	84.81
Emplo yee Info-2		8.9	40.5	29.1	20.3	1.3	69.62
Emplo yee Info-3		8.9	24.1	35.4	27.8	3.8	59.49
Org-plan&p ro-1		3.8	44.3	36.7	13.9	1.3	81.01

Org-plan&pro-2		1.3	38.0	39.2	20.3	1.3		77.22
Org-plan&pro-3		2.5	41.8	35.4	19.0	1.3		77.22
Org-plan&pro-4		7.6	43.0	36.7	8.9	3.8		79.75
Org-plan&pro-5		1.3	29.1	45.6	20.3	3.8		74.68
Client Info-1		5.1	36.7	34.2	16.5	7.6		70.89
Client Info-2		7.6	31.6	31.6	22.8	6.3		63.29
Client Info-3			32.9	36.7	24.1	6.3		69.62
General Org Info-1		2.5	39.2	36.7	19.0	2.5		75.95
General Org Info-2		7.6	34.2	40.5	16.5	1.3		74.68
General Org Info-3		5.1	34.2	44.3	13.9	2.5		78.48
General Org Info-4		2.5	31.6	36.7	27.8	1.3		68.35
								1105.06
Average								**73.67**

23

Chart-3 of Table-8b: Respondents' Ratings on Information Types

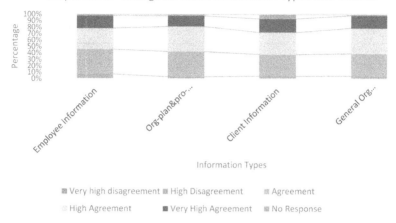

Respondents' Ratings on Broad Information Types Sub-Classes

■ Very high disagreement ■ High Disagreement ▨ Agreement
▨ High Agreement ■ Very High Agreement ▨ No Response

Chart-4 of Table-8b: Respondents' Ratings on Information Types

Respondents' Ratings on Information Types

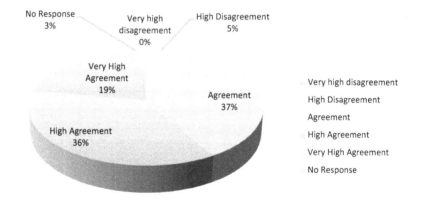

Information Types	Very high disagreement	High Disagreement	Agree ment	High Agreement	Very High Agreement	No Response
Employee Information	0	7.17	38.82	32.49	19.41	2.11
Org-plan&pro-Information	0	3.29	39.24	38.73	16.46	2.28
Client Information	0	4.22	33.76	34.18	21.10	6.75
General Org Information	0	4.43	34.81	39.56	19.30	1.90
Information Types	**0**	**4.78**	**36.66**	**36.24**	**19.07**	**3.26**

Factors Affecting in Information Sources

From the detail examination of the three charts namely Chart-5, Chart-6 & Chart-7 of Table-9 as shown in the following pages, we can find the affect in various sorts of Information Sources on information behavior. Let's, first examine and draw results from the Chart 5, which showed traditional Information Source & Related Statements. The chart indicated that major portion (i.e. in an average 70%, also see in Table-10 in the following page) of the respondents had used all available sources of information. Nevertheless, chart 5 also indicated that traditional information type 8, 9 & 11 are the three traditional information sources, which were comparatively not much used as compared to other traditional information sources. Regarding non-respondent, there were in an average 5% only (see in Table-10 in the following page) in all sorts of available sources of traditional information, which had not significantly influence in the study. Hence, we can draw conclusion that, traditional information types 1 to 7 and 10 could have significant impact on information behaviour of NCS Officers/Managers. Nevertheless compare to above, traditional information sources 8, 9 & 11 could have only little significant impact on information behaviour of NCS Officers/Managers.

In the case of Chart 6, which showed electronic information Source & Related Statements, also found that higher portion (i.e. in an average 67%, also refer to Table-10) of the respondents had used all available sources of information. However, electronic information Source 5, 1, 9 & 2 as shown in the chart are the four electronic information sources, which were comparatively not much used as compared to other electronic information sources. Regarding non-respondent, there were in an average 4% (see in Table-10) in most of available sources of electronic information. This means, the influence in the study were not significant. Nevertheless, in the case of electronic source-3, which has 22% (see in Table-9 in the following page) non-respondent, could have significant influence in the study. After considering and comparing the facts and figures explained above, we can draw conclusion that more than 50% of available sources of electronic information (i.e. 3, 4, 6, 7 & 8) could have significant impact on information behaviour of NCS Officers/Managers. But compare to above, electronic information sources 5, 1, 9 & 2 could have only little significant impact on information behaviour of NCS Officers/Managers.

Similarly in the case of Chart 7, which showed personal information source & related statements, again found that greater portion (i.e. in an average 81%, also refer to Table-10) of the respondents had used all available sources of personal information. However, personal information source 5, 4, & 2 as shown in the chart are the three personal information sources, which were not much used (i.e. in between 20% - 30%, see in Table-9 also) as compared to other personal information sources. Concerning to the non-respondent, there were in an average only 2% were found (see in Table-10), hence, which influence in the study were not significant. Therefore, we can draw conclusion that, although all personal information sources were used at moderate level, personal information sources 1 and 3 could have greater significant impact on information behaviour of NCS Officers/Managers compare to personal information sources 5, 4 & 2.

The Chart 8 & 9 as shown in the following pages, which showed a broad category of three types of information source, also conformed our above results and finding, where significant portion (i.e. in an average about 73%, also refer to Table-10) of the respondents were used all available sources of information. Relating to the average percentage of non-respondent of overall information sources (i.e. traditional, electronic & personal information sources) were also found 3.5% only (see in Chart-8, Chart-9 & Table-10 also), which influence in the study were not significant. Thus, it can be concluded and generalised that, all three type of information sources might have significant impact on information behaviour of Nepalese Civil Services Officers/Managers.

Chart-5 of Table-9: Respondents' Ratings on Traditional Information Source & Related Statements

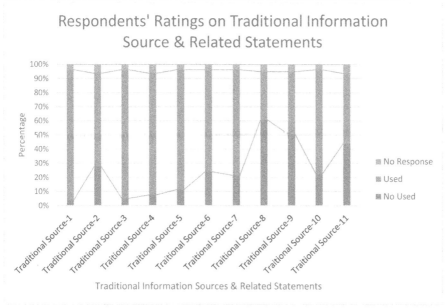

27

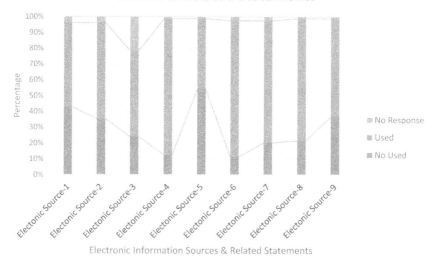

Respondents' Ratings on Electronic Information Source & Related Statements

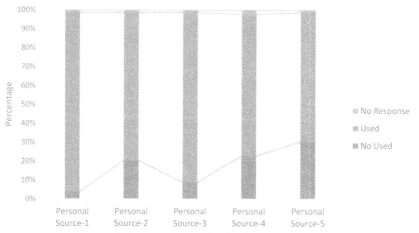

Respondents' Ratings on Personal Information Source & Related Statements

Chart-8 of Table-10: Respondents' Ratings on Information Sources

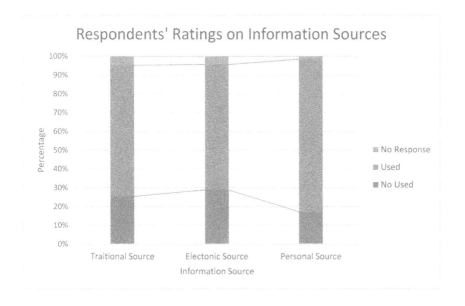

Respondents' Ratings on Information Sources

Table-9: Percentage of Sources of Information

Information Source	Percentage		
	No Used	Used	No Response
Traditional Source-1	4	92	4
Traditional Source-2	28	66	6
Traditional Source-3	5	91	4
Traditional Source-4	8	86	6
Traditional Source-5	11	85	4
Traditional Source-6	24	72	4
Traditional Source-7	22	75	4
Traditional Source-8	61	34	5
Traditional Source-9	51	44	5
Traditional Source-10	23	73	4
Traditional Source-11	44	49	6
Electonic Source-1	43	53	4
Electonic Source-2	35	61	4
Electonic Source-3	24	54	22
Electonic Source-4	13	86	1
Electonic Source-5	54	44	1
Electonic Source-6	11	86	3
Electonic Source-7	20	77	3
Electonic Source-8	22	77	1
Electonic Source-9	37	62	1
Personal Source-1	4	95	1
Personal Source-2	20	78	1
Personal Source-3	9	90	1
Personal Source-4	23	75	3
Personal Source-5	30	68	1

Chart-9 of Table-10: Respondents' Ratings on Information Source

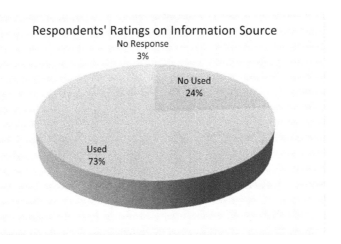

Respondents' Ratings on Information Source

Table-10: Percentage of Sources of Information

Information Source	Average Percentage		
	No Used	Used	No Response
Traditional Source	25	70	5
Electonic Source	29	67	4
Personal Source	17	81	2
Information Source	71	218	11
Information Source	23.8	72.6	3.5

Inferential Analysis of Data

In the inferential analysis, we have attempted to explore the knowledge of the relationship among variables, identify statistically significant differences and among different sub-groups of independent and dependent variables, and so on. For these objectives, multivariate analysis of variance (MANOVA), analysis of variance (ANOVA), and multiple comparisons with the Scheffe test were carried out to test our hypothesis.

Interpretation of the Results of Multivariate Test:

Using the Multivariate Tests, researcher first attempted to examine whether the difference among those variables are statistically significant or not.

Let's examine the results of MANOVA test Table-3 as shown in the following page. After examining the results of the **Table-3: Multivariate Tests (Pillai's Trace)** in the **Sig**. column, we found that all our independent variables' significant values are lesser than our cut-off point significant level 0.05. These figures suggested that the differences are statistically significant in all six independent variables (i.e. gender, age, education, management class/level, job experience, information system use at work). Now the next step is to conduct ANOVA test on all these six independent variables again in other to test the magnitude of the different.

Table-3: Multivariate Tests (Pillai's Trace)

S. No.	Effect		Value	F	Hypothesis df	Error df	Sig.	Partial Eta Squared
1	A2	Gender	.868	11.936^b	11.000	20.000	.000*	.868
2	A3	Age	1.133	2.496	22.000	42.000	.005*	.567
3	A6	Class	.704	4.330^b	11.000	20.000	.002*	.704
4	A7	Edu_Degree	1.163	2.652	22.000	42.000	.003*	.581
5	A8	Total Service Years	1.928	1.945	44.000	92.000	.004*	.482
6	A10	Level of IS used at work	2.216	5.654	33.000	66.000	.000*	.739
	* Sig. At ≤ 0.05;							
	Note:- The table format of the SPSS OUTPUT has been slightly modified for the readability; Only statistically significant variables are reported in the table shown above, to economies space in the report.							

Interpretation of the Results of ANOVA Test:

ANOVA analysis is useful to test whether the level/groups associated with an independent variable or a combination of independent variables are significantly different. Result shown in **Sig**. column of Table-4, as mentioned in the following page, indicated that all significant values for the mentioned independent variables are lesser than significant level 0.05. However, independent variable named as management class/level is not shown in the table. This means, the independent variable (i.e.

management class/level) did not support for Post-Hoc test as it has only two levels of each factor. According the result shown in the **Table-4** in the following page, gender variable was found statistically different in 2 information characteristics items, 1 type of information item; age variable was found statistically different in 2 information characteristics items; education level variable was found statistically different in 1 information characteristic item, and 1 type of information item; total service years variable was found statistically different in 2 information characteristic items; and in information systems used at work variable was found statistically different in 1 information characteristic item and 2 type of information items.

Now, we need to do further detail analysis of these five independent variables namely gender, age, education, job experience (or total service years), information system use at work (Level of IS used at work). For this analysis, Post-Hoc Multiple Comparisons with the Scheffe test was conducted to these 5 independent variables.

Table-4: Tests of Between-Subjects Effects

S. No.	Source Variable	Dependent Variable	Type III Sum of Squares	df	Mean Square	F	Sig.	Partial Eta Squared
A2	Gender	Flexibility	2.993	1	2.993	7.421	.011*	.198
		Truthfulness	2.872	1	2.872	8.913	.006**	.229
		Org-plan&pro-2	3.328	1	3.328	7.759	.009**	.205
A3	Age	Comparability	2.690	2	1.345	3.419	.046*	.186
		Flexibility	2.794	2	1.397	3.463	.044*	.188
A7	Edu_Degree	Usefulness	1.741	2	.870	3.327	.050*	.182
		Org-plan&pro-2	3.724	2	1.862	4.342	.022*	.224
A8	Total Service Years	Flexibility	5.222	4	1.306	3.237	.025*	.301
		Truthfulness	4.610	4	1.152	3.576	.017*	.323
A10	Level of IS used at work	Comparability	3.486	3	1.162	2.954	.048*	.228
		Employee Info-1	7.884	3	2.628	9.150	.000**	.478
		Employee Info-3	7.139	3	2.380	5.167	.005**	.341

* Sig. At ≤ 0.05;　　　　** Sig. At ≤ 0.01;

Note:- The table format of the SPSS OUTPUT has been slightly modified for the readability;
Only statistically significant variables are reported in the table shown above, to economies space in the report.

Interpretation of the Results of Post-Hoc Multiple Comparisons with the Scheffe Test:

This test was carried out to identify which of the subgroups' means differ significantly from the others variables and in what direction ($+^{tiv}$ or $-^{tiv}$) of the differences. The results from the Post-Hoc Multiple Comparisons (PHMC) with the Scheffe test were identified three independent variables (i.e. age, job experience (or total service years) and information system use at work (Level of IS used at work)), which did created differences among the sub-groups of information dimension (DV). The tables related with the detail results from the Post-Hoc Multiple Comparisons (PHMC) with the Scheffe test were not shown and explained in detail in this article due to the space limitation. However, researcher will be provided upon request for the interested readers.

7. Findings, Implication, Discussion & Conclusion

The main objective of the study is to understand the impact of personal and professional factors on information behavior of NCS Officers/Managers in GoN.

Based on the model, we empirical measured these variables applying with the three information dimension in the context of information behavior of officer/managers in the Nepalese Civil Service. After measured the information behavior of NCS officers/managers using through various statistical analysis and test, the study shows that only following variables were found significant in this study.

The Study Module after Data Analysis

This research study shows that in demographic variable age and in organisational variable job experience and information system use are only the variables, which make a difference significantly in the information dimensions. This means, therefore, both null hypothesis (H_0) and alternative hypothesis (H_1) have been only partially supported.

The Study model after data analysis

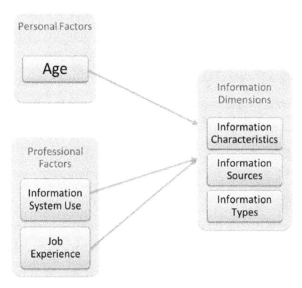

Figure 2: The Study Module after Data Analysis

Results of the ANOVA analysis indicated that all significance values for independent variables were statistically significance while interpreting the results regarding the examination of impact of independent variables in the information dimensions as carried out in this study, gender was found to do create difference in 2 information characteristics (Flexibility and Truthfulness), 1 type of information (Org. plan & procedure-Stat-2 information). Age was found to make a difference in 2 information characteristics (Flexibility and Comparability). While in education level, it was found to do create difference in 1 information characteristics (Usefulness), and 1 type of information (Org. plan & procedure-Stat-2 information). Similarly, total service years was found to make different in 2 information characteristic (Flexibility and Truthfulness). Finally, information systems used at work was found to do create different in 1 information characteristics (Comparability), and 2 type of information (Org. plan & procedure-Stat-1 & 3, information).

However, management class/level variable did not support for Post-Hoc test, as it has only two levels in the factor/variable. Thus, it is not shown in the result table. Again for more detail analysis, Post-Hoc Multiple Comparisons (PHMC) with the Scheffe test was conducted to these 5 independent variables. This test examines which of the IV subgroups' means differ significantly from the other (i.e. age, sex, education, management level, job experience and information system use at work) variables and at what direction ($+^{tiv}$ or $-^{tiv}$) of the differences and shows how these IVs (personal & professional factors) will affect in the IB or in three information dimensions (i.e. information characteristics, information sources and information types) as the DVs.

The general findings of the study identified that the three IVs (i.e. age as a personal factor, information system use and job experience as a professional factors) were found affected or impact in the information dimensions (DV) including its component variables (i.e. information characteristics, information sources and information types). Thus, the study concluded that the use of NCS Officers/Managers' age, information system use and job experience were the three IVs, which did created differences or impact in their Information Behaviour (IB), in other words, in the information dimensions (DV) including its component variables (i.e. information characteristics, information sources and information types), which is also illustrated in the *Figure 2: The Study Module after Data Analysis* above, as an updated study module after the finding of this study.

The possible reasons of these outcomes might be the cause of fewer no. of levels inclusion in sex & management level factors and fewer no. of cases collected in this research, especially in the case of education, sex and management level factors.

This empirical research findings are also compatible with the other end of empirical research that has been conducted by [Palmquist, 2006, as cited in (Almutairi, 2011)] using several variables impacting the use of different information types. From his empirical investigation, he also concluded that each group has different assumptions of what makes information useful and valuable. Finally, empirical researches that have been carried out in several different countries and contexts, including NCS in GoN also

36

showed a clear evidence that these variables play a major role in information behavior with varying degrees and magnitudes based on the countries and context/situation.

Limitation of the Study

Due to resource and time constraints, only 155 officers of NCS were approached to get data. Thus, the low sample size is one of the major limitations of this study. In addition, data were collected from Kathmandu Valley only. The research can be healthier by getting data from several cities, regions and also by obtaining more sample sizes.

Future Research Directions

While doing this type of research in future, researchers should be aware that differences in patterns of one's information behavior might encapsulate the impact of other variables like demographic and organizational variables, on their behavior. It is because, the chaotic nature of information behaviour is a tip off the complexity of the environment and hence, postulates to include more variables in our study to explain this behaviour. Therefore, author advice that the upcoming future researchers should build comprehensive relational models so that it will contribute to enhance our knowledge of the more factors that enhance or hinder the efficiency and effectiveness of managers' information behavior by incorporating additional factors like, discipline, profession, work task, specialization, career stage, geographic location, situation, individual, organization & social role, demographic groupings and other context and so on, in the context of Nepalese organisations and Nepalese Civil Services. Beside that information behaviour should be examined in term of how these different context level interact with each other and how these interaction affects information behaviour.

***

References

Almutairi, H. (2011). Factors affecting the information behaviour of managers in the Kuwaiti civil ervice: A relational model. *Information Research, 16*(2), 477.

Ashill, N. J., & Jobber, D. (2001). Defining the information needs of senior marketing executives: An exploratory study. *Qualitative Market Study, 4*(1), 52-61.

Auster, E., & Choo, C. (1993). Environmental scanning by CEOs in two Canadian industries. *Journal of the American Society for Information Science, 44*(4), 194-203.

Bates, M. J. (2010). *Information Behavior In Encyclopedia of Library and Information Sciences, 3rd Ed.* (Vol. 3). (M. J. Bates, & M. N. Maack, Eds.) New York: CRC Press.

Breen, H. (2005). Assessing the information needs of Australian gaming managers. *UNLV Gaming Research & Review Journal, 9*(2), 29-43.

Bystrom, K. (2006). Information activities in work tasks. In K. E. Fisher, S. Erdelez, & L. McKechnie (Eds.), *Theories of information behavior* (pp. 174-178). Medford, NJ: Information Today.

Case, D. O. (2006). Information behavior. *Annual Review of Information Science and Technology, 40*(1), 293-327. Retrieved from https://liswiki.org/wiki/Information_behavior_theories

Case, D. O. (2007). *Looking for Information: A Survey of Research on Information Seeking, Needs, and Behavior* (2 ed.). Amsterdam: Elsevier. Retrieved from https://liswiki.org/wiki/Information_behavior_theories

Hansen, P. (2006). Work task'information-seeking and retrieval processes. In K. E. Fisher, S. Erdelez, & L. McKechnie (Eds.), *Theories of information behavior* (pp. 392-6). Medfort, NJ: Information Today.

Hupfer, M. E., & Detlor, B. (2006). Gender and Web information seeking: a self-concepts orientation model. *Journal of the American Society for Information Science and Technology, 57*(8), 1105-1115.

Koksal, M. H. (2008). How expert marketing research affects company export performance. *Marketing Intelligence & Planning, 26*(4), 416-430.

Leckie, G. J., Pettigrew, K. E., & Sylvain, C. (1996). Modeling the information seeking of professionals: A general model derived from research on engineers, health care professionals, and lawyers. *The Library Quarterly: Information, Community, Policy, 66*(2), 161-193. Retrieved from http://www.jstor.org/stable/4309109

Lorence, D., & Park, H. (2007). Gender and online heath information: a partitioned technology assessment. *Heath Information and Libraries Journal, 24*(3), 204-209.

O'Reilly, C. A. (1982). Variations in decision makers' use of information sources: The impact of quality and accessibility of information. *Academy of Management Journal, 25*(4), 756-771.

Paisley, W. J. (1968). Information needs and users. *Annual Review of Information Science and Technology, 3*, 1-30.

Palsdottir, A. (2003). Icelandic citizens' everyday life health information behavior. *Health Informatics Journal, 9*(4), 225-40.

Robinson, M. A. (2010). An empirical analysis of engineers' information behaviors. *Journal of the American Society for Information Science and Technology, 61*(4), 640–658. doi:10.1002/asi.21290

Savolainen, R. (2007). Information behavior and information practice: Reviewing the 'umbrella concepts' of information-seeking studies. *The Library Quarterly,*

77(2), 109-27. Retrieved from
https://liswiki.org/wiki/Information_behavior_theories

Simon, H. (1960). *The New Science of Management Decision.* New York, NY:
Harper.

Sudin, S. (2011). Fairness of and satisfaction with performance appraisal process.
*2nd International Conference on Business and Economic Research (2nd Icber
2011) Proceeding.* Pahang. Retrieved Feb. 2017, from
https://ideas.repec.org/a/grg/03mngt/v2y2011i1p66-83.html

Swanson, L. (2003). An information-processing model of maintenance management.
International Journal of Production Economics, 83(1), 45-64.

Thompson, J. D. (1967). *Organizations in Action.* New York, NY: McGraw-Hill.

Urquhart, C., & Yeoman, A. (2009). Information behavior of women: theoretical
perspectives on gender. *Journal of Documentation, 66*(1), 113-139.

Williams, D., & Coles, L. (2007). Evidence-based practice in teaching: an
information perspective. *Journal of Documentation, 63*(6), 812-35.

Wilson, T. (1981). On user studies and information needs. *Journal of Documentation
, 37*(1), 3-15. Retrieved from
http://www.informationr.net/tdw/publ/papers/1981infoneeds.html

Wilson, T. (1999). Models in information behaviour research. *Journal of
Documentation, 55*(3), 249-70. Retrieved from
http://informationr.net/tdw/publ/papers/1999JDoc.html

Wilson, T. D. (2000). Human information behavior. *Special Issue on Information
Science Research, 3*(2), 49-55. Retrieved from
https://www.researchgate.net/publication/270960171_Human_Information_Be
havior

***

About the authors

Binaya Hari Maskey is a doctoral candidate in the Sai Nath University, Ranchi (Jharkhand), India, under the self-scholarship from Nepal. He holds M.B.A. from T.U., Kathmandu, Nepal and P.G.D. in Information Systems from Brighton University, Brighton, U.K. He is a faculty staff of Public Service Training Department at Nepal Administrative Staff College (NASC), Jawalakhel, Nepal. This research has been funded by Research and Consultancy Services Department (RCSD), Nepal Administrative Staff College (NASC). He can be contacted at: bhmaskey@gmail.com OR binaya.maskey@nasc.org.np .

Peer Reviewed by:

Dr. Jyoti Koirala, get2jyoti@gmail.com, 9843473088

Dr. Suman Acharya, sumantext@gmail.com, 9841322275

*****

Publisher: Eliva Press SRL

Email: info@elivapress.com

Eliva Press is an independent publishing house established for the publication and dissemination of academic works all over the world. Company provides high quality and professional service for all of our authors.

Our Services:
Free of charge, open-minded, eco-friendly, innovational.

-Free standard publishing services (manuscript review, step-by-step book preparation, publication, distribution, and marketing).
-No financial risk. The author is not obliged to pay any hidden fees for publication.
-Editors. Dedicated editors will assist step by step through the projects.
-Money paid to the author for every book sold. Up to 50% royalties guaranteed.
-ISBN (International Standard Book Number). We assign a unique ISBN to every Eliva Press book.
-Digital archive storage. Books will be available online for a long time. We don't need to have a stock of our titles. No unsold copies. Eliva Press uses environment friendly print on demand technology that limits the needs of publishing business. We care about environment and share these principles with our customers.
-Cover design. Cover art is designed by a professional designer.
-Worldwide distribution. We continue expanding our distribution channels to make sure that all readers have access to our books.

www.elivapress.com

www.ingramcontent.com/pod-product-compliance
Lightning Source LLC
Chambersburg PA
CBHW070903070326
40690CB00009B/1976